THE GOODNESS OF
BEANS
PEAS AND
LENTILS

· · · · · · · · · ·

JOHN MIDGLEY

Illustrated by

IAN SIDAWAY

RANDOM HOUSE
NEW YORK

ACKNOWLEDGEMENTS
The author thanks Sue Midgley and Jo Swinnerton for
kindly checking the text, and Penny Casas for
her generous permission to reproduce a recipe.

FURTHER READING
For those interested in reading more about food and health
The Food Pharmacy, by Jean Carper (Simon and Schuster) and
Superfoods, by Michael Van Straten and
Barbara Griggs (Dorling Kindersley)
are recommended. Harold McGee's *On Food and Cooking*
(Harper Collins) and Reay Tannahill's *Food in History*
(Penguin) are also highly recommended.

Published in the United States by Random House, Inc., New York.

This work was originally published in Great Britain by
Pavilion Books Limited, London.

Library of Congress Cataloging-in-Publication Data

Midgley, John.
The goodness of beans/John Midgley; illustrated by Ian Sidaway.
p. cm. – (The Goodness of)
ISBN 0-679-41624-2
1. Cookery (Beans) 2. Beans – Utilization. 3. Beans – Health
aspects. I. Title. II. Series: Midgley, John. Goodness of.
TX803.B4M54 1992
641.6'565 – dc20 92-13768

Manufactured in Belgium

2 4 6 8 9 7 5 3

First U.S. edition

CONTENTS
. . . .

PART ONE
· · · · · · · · · ·

BEANS, PEAS AND LENTILS
· · · · · · · · · ·

Beans and peas are the edible seeds of leguminous plants, a large group of flowering plants that produce double-seamed pods with a single row of seeds. Belonging to this group are the garden and field peas, the chick pea (or garbanzo), the mangetout (snow pea), and the sugar snap pea, as well as the broad (fava) bean, and the mung, soy, aduki, black-eyed, lima, runner, and many varieties of *phaseolus vulgaris*, or the haricot (navy) bean, which is native to Central America but now common in many different parts of the world.

Native to southern Asia or the northern Middle East, the lentil belongs to the same family, but even in their fresh state lentils are much harder seeds and need long cooking. Lentils are always sold dried and come in a dazzling array of colours, from olive green and brown to red and yellow varieties; the most prized are grown in the volcanic soil of le Puy in the Massif Central region of France. Dried legumes, including whole or split peas, chick peas, the mature and dried seeds of fresh beans and other, more exotic beans such as urd and toor dal are collectively known in Great Britain as 'pulses'.

Okra is not strictly a legume; the pod is seamless and carries a double row of seeds and the plant is an hibiscus, related to cotton. However, okra recipes have been included because the vegetable resembles fresh green beans and is often cooked in similar ways.

Although most beans can produce sprouts from fresh seeds, the most commonly available sprouts are from mung and alfalfa beans. (Sprouted mung beans are the most common, usually sold loose or in plastic bags in supermarkets and Asian stores and are labelled as 'bean sprouts'.)

Some fresh legumes

Peas
Garden pea
Mangetout, or snow pea
Petit pois
Sugar snap pea

Beans
Black-eyed bean
Broad, or fava bean
Lima bean
Runner bean
Borlotto bean
Wax, or yellow bean

Some dried legumes

Beans
Aduki bean
Black-eyed bean
Broad, or fava bean
Borlotto bean
Boston, haricot, or navy bean
Large haricot, or navy bean
Cannellino bean
Black kidney bean
Red kidney bean
White kidney bean
Flageolet bean
Pinto bean
Ful medames
Lima bean
Mung bean
Pigeon pea, or toor dal
Black soy bean
Fermented black soy bean
Yellow soy bean
Rice bean
Urd bean

Peas
Chick pea
Dried pea
Green split pea
Yellow split pea

Lentils
Brown lentil
Large and small green lentils
Red lentil
Puy lentil
Yellow lentil

Growing peas and beans

A comfortable man, with dividends,
And the first salmon and the first green peas.
H. W. LONGFELLOW

As the poet intimated, there are few more exquisite and fleeting luxuries than the first garden peas of summer. Because peas *(pisum sativum)* very rapidly lose their sweetness and soon become mealy, really fresh garden peas are somewhat difficult to come by. (Sensibly, many people prefer good quality frozen peas to the tough bullets that so often masquerade as 'fresh' peas.) Eating the perfect fresh garden pea is a pleasure often denied to the non gardener. Peas are a little tricky to grow, are prone to attack by pests and diseases, and are unproductive in relation to the space they occupy. They are grown from seed sown from winter to early spring in rows, in rich, well-drained soil. They require regular watering and the seedlings must be trained on vertical supports. They are harvested from late spring to midsummer, as soon as the pods have reached their full length and feel properly swollen. Mangetouts (snow peas) are grown in the same way but are harvested before the pods lengthen and the seeds swell.

Broad (fava) beans *(vicia fava)* are grown for their

fleshy cream- or green-coloured seeds, and are best when no larger than the ball of a thumb. The only beans native to Europe, they are grown by planting seeds in rows (allowing plenty of space between seeds and rows), in fertile, well-drained soil. The plants are usually supported within an enclosure constructed with border stakes tied together with string. The plants' growing tops are pinched out when the pods are partly developed, to divert energy to the maturing seeds. The pods are harvested as required. Seeds sown in early spring will be ready from early to midsummer.

French beans *(phaseolus vulgaris)* come in many different varieties with green, yellow, purple or white pods. Their longstanding popularity in France, where the many new varieties have been developed, has earned them their name. Haricot (navy) beans are the mature seeds, allowed to develop on the plant and eaten fresh or dried. Flageolet beans are the same seeds, sold at an intermediate stage, before they have dried completely. Otherwise, the pods are generally harvested before the seeds mature. The dwarf varieties do not need staking and can even be grown in tubs, whereas

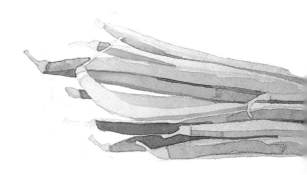

the climbers will need vertical support once the seedlings have grown to a height of about 10cm/4 inches. The plants are not hardy, and seeds should be sown wide apart in rows after the danger of frost has passed, preferably in a sunny and sheltered position, in well-drained soil. They are fast to mature and should start to crop two months from sowing.

If french beans are identified with France, then the runner bean *(phaseolus multiflorus)* deserves to be called the Englishman's bean. Also called scarlet runners by virtue of their flowers, they are grown for summer and early autumn crops, succeeding french beans. Relatively easy to cultivate successfully, they require vertical support and plenty of moisture in dry weather, applied both to the roots and to the foliage. The growing tips are pinched out to encourage flowering side shoots, and picking itself encourages the plants to produce more pods. Seeds are sown wide apart in rows and trained on to canes or netting. Somewhat coarse in texture, runner beans should be picked young, before the seeds mature in the pods. They are usually topped, tailed, and sliced before cooking.

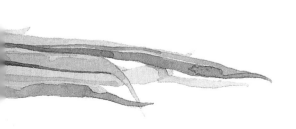

THE GOODNESS OF BEANS, PEAS AND LENTILS
· · · · · · · · · ·

The main practical benefit of these vegetables is their protein content, double that of grains. When paired with starch or grain, beans, peas and lentils offer the best balance of essential amino acids and a particularly rich supply of protein. Many of the world's traditional cuisines have understood this intuitively. Venetian rice with peas; a paella of rice and chick peas from the Levante region of Spain; the ancient Greek dish of pasta with chick peas that is still prepared today in the deep south of Italy; Mexican re-fried beans with corn tortillas; Tex-Mex chilli con carne with rice; Southern hopping John; and Tuscan *pasta e fagioli* are just some examples.

For centuries, Indian vegetarians have combined legumes with carbohydrates (rice and breads), other fresh vegetables, herbs and spices, fat, and dairy products such as yoghurt to produce a balanced diet that delivers all the important nutrients. Other traditional societies in different parts of the world have long valued beans in the diet, especially if meat and fish have been scarce, and perhaps none more than the Chinese and Japanese, for whom the soy bean is quite indispensable. Not only is it the richest source of protein (equal to prime meat, weight for weight), this amazing bean is also extremely versatile. It can be preserved and fermented whole with salt, or fermented to make a kind of cheese, processed to make curd, or sprouted, and is an essential ingredient in many bottled or canned flavouring sauces and pastes, such as soy sauce, yellow and black bean sauces, chilli bean sauce and hoisin sauce.

Beans are an excellent source of minerals, especially iron, as well as B vitamins and vitamins A and C, in their fresh forms, and dietary fibre. Without adequate fibre in the diet, the bowel is at greater risk of developing cancer. It is now widely accepted that the high incidence of colon cancers in Great Britain and the USA is closely associated with insufficient dietary fibre. Put crudely, fecal bulk is healthy and beans and other high-fibre foods promote regular, softer, and bulkier bowel movements. Some researchers suspect that beans may contain cancer-blocking substances, too.

Soluble fibre from beans also appears to ferment in the gut, and the ensuing bacterial action may be implicated in lowering harmful LDL (low density lipoprotein) cholesterol in the blood, thus protecting the cardiovascular system. There is considerable evidence that bean-eaters and vegetarians have lower blood pressure, perhaps because of the lower levels of LDL cholesterol that beans and plant fibre appear to promote. Dried beans are also recommended to diabetics because they barely raise blood-sugar levels, although commercially canned beans that are high in sugar may be damaging because they raise blood-sugar levels.

Constipation is another common complaint, particularly among the elderly. Eating beans regularly will swiftly remedy constipation. Haemorrhoids is an unpleasant condition that is exacerbated by constipation and sufferers should benefit from beans in the diet.

The bean effect: 'an ill wind behind' (Dr Johnson), or a breath of fresh air?

Beans, beans, they're good for the heart;
The more you eat, the more you . . .
A POPULAR CHILDREN'S RHYMING REFRAIN

Beanes are harde of digestion,
and make troblesum dreames
TURNER

There is no doubt that beans, peas and lentils, especially in dried form, provoke not a little flatulence in those unaccustomed to them. This has been noted periodically in history; vernacular and literary jokes about farting are as old as the hills. So are taboos against public emissions, dating back at least to Roman times, when public farting was outlawed. Allied to these sensible prohibitions was a curious belief that beans induced lechery, perhaps through association with the ribald drunkenness characterizing the type of exhibitionist who enjoys making loud posterior reports expressly to scandalize the company. Breaking wind has also been considered a healthy activity, perhaps on the principle of 'better out than in', but what is it about beans that causes the problem? It is their indigestibility because of the presence of certain sugar molecules, as Harold McGee explains in his book, *On Food and Cooking*. What happens is that the molecules survive their passage through the upper intestine intact, only to be subjected to bacterial attack in the lower intestine, of which gas is the waste product. In general, beans that are properly cooked give less trouble, and fresh beans less still.

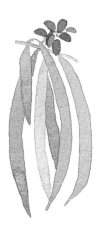

LEGUMES IN HISTORY

Beans and folklore

It was once believed that the perfume of bean flowers could intoxicate, hence the euphemism 'beans are in flower' that used to be uttered if someone acted in a silly or mad fashion. According to an old European custom, a bean would be concealed in Twelfth Night cakes and the title of Bean King was awarded to the child who found the bean in his or her portion of cake. Beans are synonymous with health and the phrase 'full of beans' was originally used to describe fresh and highly spirited horses, then loosely extended to humans. Beans are an old form of currency, although the phrases 'haven't a bean' and 'not worth a bean' probably stem from the French *biens*, meaning property or goods. It is interesting to speculate as to the origin of the English colloquial endearment, 'old bean', which was once enormously popular but has now all but vanished from usage.

Etymology

Our word bean derives from Old Norse *baun*. Lentil comes from Latin *lens* and the optical lens is so-called because the first were lentil-shaped, having two convex sides, viewed sideways. Our peas, in common with Italian *piselli* and French *pois* derive from the Latin word for the vegetable, *pisum*. Chick pea was originally *ciche pease* in English, deriving, like Italian *ceci* and Catalan *cigron*, from Latin *cicer*. (The Castilian Spanish word *garbanzo*, on the other hand, has a Greek root.) The Castilian and Italian names of the broad (fava) bean (*haba* and *fava*) stem from the Latin word for this European vegetable, *fava*.

A brief history of beans, peas and lentils

The wild parents of beans, peas and lentils and other vegetables were gathered by our earliest ancestors to supplement their diet of game or fish. After the first settlements grew up around fields of wild grain in the Near East, and early civilizations learned to grow their food, so lentils, peas, chick peas and broad (fava) beans became domesticated, starting as far back as *c.*7000 BC. The lentil is thought to be the oldest legume to have been cultivated, whereas the pea spread quickly eastward and westward from its native Middle East. The field pea was probably cultivated by early civilizations in what is today Thailand, and traces of the vegetable have been excavated in the Indus plain sites of Mohenjo-Daro and Harappa.

In the western hemisphere, the Indians of Central America had learned first to gather, then, in Peru around 5000 BC, to grow beans of the *phaseolus* varieties. Around 2500 BC, the Sumerian civilization cultivated chick peas, lentils and broad beans, along with onions, leeks, garlic, and other vegetables. Broad beans, peas, chick peas and lentils were eaten by the Egyptians, the Greeks, and the Romans, who noticed that the plants did not exhaust the soil they were grown in. As Harold McGee has observed, the Romans must have valued legumes very highly if several distinguished Roman citizens were named after them (Fabius from *fava*, Cicero from *cicer*, Piso from *pisum* and Lentulus from *lens*.) The Romans introduced peas to the rest of Europe. The traditional English pease pudding may date back to the Dark Ages, when cooking often consisted of keeping a cauldron continuously on the boil, replenished from time to time with whatever ingredients were to hand. The monastic vegetable gardens ensured a supply of fresh and dried broad beans and peas for the many meatless days of the calendar. Secular plots also grew broad beans, peas and lentils, which were eaten with grain, and supplied much of the protein in the medieval diet and helped to neutralize the very high salt content of food at that time. Typical dishes might have included bean soups and puréed peas or broad beans with bacon, a combination

that survives in many traditional European recipes today. So important were broad beans, especially in the Mediterranean countries, that an anaemic condition (favism) that is caused by eating undercooked beans is named after them. Susceptibility to the disease appears to be genetically transmitted and cases still occur in the Mediterranean region.

India, a country of many vegetarians, has long grown lentils, peas, chick peas, and the native mung bean, and long ago its people learned how to make dried peas and lentils more digestible by cooking them with ginger, turmeric and other spices. These dried seed vegetables (*dals*) are often split (*dal* is an old word meaning 'divided'). The nutritive value of the Indian vegetarian diet, which combines beans with rice or grains, fresh vegetables and dairy products, has already been noted.

Further east, the early Chinese grew and later learned to develop a range of by-products of the highly productive soy bean, which is native to northern China. Soy sauce, bean curd, and fermented, preserved black soy beans date back to around 200 BC but may well have existed several centuries earlier. Later centuries saw the invention of soy bean oil, soy flour and a variety of soy bean sauces and pastes.

Meanwhile, in Europe, the Carthaginians brought chick peas with them to Spain, where to this day they remain an important food, particularly for the rural poor; in Castilian Spanish, 'chick pea-eater' is a term reserved for the most humble individual. The Spaniards discovered the *phaseolus* varieties of beans on landing in Central America and later the lima bean, a close relative, on reaching Peru; they also introduced the European legumes to that hemisphere. These new, edible bean pods and their mature, fresh, or dried beans were adopted enthusiastically in the Old World.

The Puritan settlers brought the bean back from the Old World to the New. Their main meal on the

Sabbath was Boston baked beans, prepared the previous day and left to cook slowly on the hearth fire. In fact, one-pot meals of pork and beans are an old tradition that the English Puritans inherited from medieval times. The dish was finally marketed internationally by the firm of Heinz, whose technologists developed a recipe for pork and beans in tomato sauce suitable for canning. In North America today, the soy bean is the most important cash crop, first planted in 1854 for its oil and protein content. The USA now produces about 75 per cent of the global soy bean crop, mostly for soy meal, an exceptionally effective animal feed.

The recipes have been inspired by traditional cuisines of many parts of the world and are intended to serve four, unless otherwise indicated.

black   blackeye   butter

lentil   puy   red lentil

turtle   yellow lentil

haricot

cannelini   chick   flageol

PART
TWO
· · · · · · · · · ·

bean mix   stew mix

GREEN BEAN SALAD

· · · · · · · · · · ·

Here is a really simple and delicious way to enjoy fresh green beans. Serve them as an appetizer or accompaniment.

450g/1lb green beans
2 cloves of garlic, peeled and finely chopped
extra virgin olive oil, to taste
juice of a lemon
salt
1 tbs fresh chives, washed and chopped

Top and tail the beans. Boil in salted water for about 5 minutes and refresh them in cold water. Dry them well with a paper towel.

Combine the beans with the remaining ingredients, mix well, and serve.

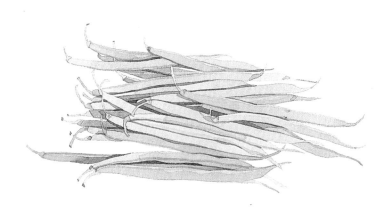

CANNELLINI BEAN SALAD

A delicious recipe by Penny Casas for a cold bean salad, taken from her book, *Tapas*. Canned beans work very well.

800g/1³/₄ lb canned cannellini beans, rinsed
1 fresh tomato, washed and diced
1 hard-boiled (hard-cooked) egg, quartered
4 stoned (pitted) black olives, quartered
1 tbs fresh parsley, washed and chopped
1 fl oz/2 tbs fruity olive oil
1 tbs white wine vinegar
salt
1 clove garlic, peeled and mashed to a paste

In a bowl, gently combine the beans, tomato, egg, olives, and parsley. In a separate bowl, whisk the oil, vinegar, salt, and garlic. Fold this into the bean mixture and marinate in the fridge for several hours.

BROAD BEAN SALAD
· · · · · · · · · · ·

The broad (fava) bean is the only true bean native to the western hemisphere and has been cultivated for thousands of years. Although commonly eaten in its dried form, this recipe is for a delightfully simple summer salad of fresh, shelled broad beans. When fresh broad beans are out of season, substitute two 425g/15oz cans of cooked cannellini beans.

900g/2lb fresh broad beans
2 cloves of garlic, peeled and finely chopped
2 spring onions (scallions), washed and thinly sliced
2 fresh tomatoes, washed and finely diced
110ml/4fl oz/$^1/_2$ cup extra virgin olive oil
1fl oz/2 tbs red wine vinegar
salt
freshly milled black pepper
fresh parsley, dill, mint, or fennel fronds

String and shell the beans. Bring a pan of salted water to the boil, immerse the beans and boil them until tender, about 35 minutes. Drain and put them on a plate or in a bowl. Mix in the garlic, spring onions, and tomatoes.

Beat the oil with the vinegar and seasoning and pour the dressing over the beans while they are still hot. Sprinkle with the fresh herbs and allow the salad to cool. Serve it at room temperature.

PUREE OF CANNELLINI BEANS
. . . .

Beans make satisfying purées, whether to accompany meat or fish or to enjoy with bread. The results of preparing this recipe with canned beans were so good that to use dry beans, which require long periods of soaking and boiling seems pointlessly time-consuming.

1 large potato, peeled
1 cup rocket leaves
800g/1³/₄lb canned cannellini beans, rinsed
110ml/4fl oz/¹/₂ cup extra virgin olive oil
2 cloves of garlic, peeled
sprigs of thyme, sage, and rosemary
350ml/12fl oz/1¹/₂ cups water
110g/4oz piece of parmesan, grated
salt
freshly milled black pepper
1 tbs olive oil
2 small, dried chilli peppers, crumbled
2 cloves of garlic, peeled and finely chopped

Bring a small pan of water to the boil and put in the potato. Boil until soft, about 20 minutes. Before removing the potato, immerse the rocket leaves and boil them for 2 minutes. Drain well.

Meanwhile, sauté the beans with 2fl oz/4 tbs of the oil, 2 cloves of garlic and the herbs for 5 minutes. Add the water and cook until it evaporates, about 15 minutes. Remove the herbs and mash the beans and garlic in the pan with the potato, adding the parmesan and 2fl oz/4 tbs of oil. Season well.

Heat 1 tbs oil in a pan and add the chilli, chopped garlic, and rocket. Heat through.

Reheat the purée briefly and divide it between four bowls. Divide the rocket into four portions and cover the purée with it. Dribble a little more oil over each and serve.

GREEN BEANS WITH PARMESAN
· · · · · · · · · · ·

This quick dish can be made with any dwarf variety of the green bean: french or matchstick beans, or even the yellow or white varieties that are sometimes available in good vegetable markets. They are lightly boiled in salted water, drained, and sprinkled with parmesan to be finished under the grill (broiler). Serve as a vegetable accompaniment.

450g/1lb green beans
50g/2oz butter, diced
50g/2oz piece of parmesan, grated
2 tbs split blanched almonds, lightly toasted and chopped
freshly milled black pepper

Pre-heat a grill.

Top and tail the beans and put them into a pot of boiling salted water. Return to the boil and cook for 3–4 minutes. Drain and transfer to a shallow ovenproof dish. Dot with butter and sprinkle with parmesan and almonds. Season well and put under the grill to melt the butter and cheese. Remove when the topping begins to turn golden.

GREEN BEANS IN TOMATO SAUCE

A delicious and very versatile accompaniment that suits almost anything.

450g/1lb green beans
1fl oz/2 tbs olive oil
1 dried red chilli pepper
3 cloves of garlic, peeled and chopped
3 ripe fresh or canned tomatoes, finely chopped
pinch of sugar
handful of fresh parsley or coriander (cilantro), washed
and chopped
salt
freshly milled black pepper

Top and tail the beans. Boil them in salted water for 3 minutes (french beans), 2 minutes (matchstick beans). Refresh in cold water and drain them well.

Heat the oil in a pan and add the chilli pepper and garlic. Stir for 1 minute taking care not to burn them, then add the tomatoes, sugar, herbs, and beans. Stir for 2 more minutes, season, and serve.

HUMMUS

· · · · · · · · · · ·

Although it can be blended with *tahina* (sesame paste), this simpler version of chick peas puréed with olive oil and lemon juice, popular in Turkey and throughout the Middle East, is delicious and authentic.

2 large cloves of garlic, peeled and halved
1 tbs olive oil
400g/14 oz can of chick peas, drained and rinsed
3fl oz/6 tbs fresh lemon juice
110ml/4fl oz/$^1/_2$ cup extra virgin olive oil
2 tsp cumin seeds, ground
1fl oz/2 tbs water
$^1/_2$ tsp cayenne
1 tbs fresh coriander (cilantro)

Heat 1 tbs of olive oil, add the garlic and fry for about 1 minute. Do not allow the garlic to brown. Remove and combine it in a food processor with the rest of the ingredients except the cayenne and coriander. Blend to a soft paste. Divide between four bowls, dress with additional olive oil to taste, sprinkle with cayenne and coriander. Serve with crudités and warm pitta bread.

YELLOW SPLIT PEA DAL
· · · · · · · · · · ·

The Indian name for this dish, *Chana dal* is also the name of the yellow split peas that are its main ingredient. Ordinary yellow split peas are equally good. Serve with a single or mixed vegetable curry and plain rice or Indian nan or chapatti breads (or substitute pitta bread).

225g/8oz *chana dal* or yellow split peas
840ml/1½ pints water
2cm/1 inch piece of fresh ginger, peeled and finely chopped
2 bay leaves
1 tsp salt
1 tsp ground turmeric
½ tsp cayenne
2 tsp *garam masala*
3fl oz/6 tbs vegetable oil
small onion, peeled and thinly sliced
2cm/1 inch piece of ginger, peeled and finely chopped
2 cloves of garlic, peeled and finely chopped
2 fresh green chillies, washed and thinly sliced

Bring the split peas and the water to a boil, skimming off the froth as it rises. After a few minutes, add the chopped ginger, bay leaves, salt, turmeric, and cayenne. Partly cover and simmer over a low heat for 1½ hours, stirring often. After 1 hour, stir in 1 tsp of the *garam masala*, made as follows:

Garam masala

Pound in a mortar or grind in a coffee grinder the following dry spices: 4 cloves, 1 tsp cumin seeds, 2cm/1 inch stick of cinnamon, 1 tsp fennel seeds, seeds from 1 tsp cardamom pods, 2 tsp coriander seeds.

Heat the oil and throw in the onion, ginger, garlic and green chillies. Allow the onion to brown a little and pour the contents over the *dal*. Stir in the remaining *garam masala* and serve.

Similar *dals* can be made in much the same way, substituting other split peas or split lentils. Whole dried beans, such as red kidney beans and black eyed beans are not strictly *dal*, but can also be cooked in the same spices after having been soaked overnight. Adjust the cooking times accordingly: lentils, for example, normally cook in under 45 minutes, while larger, dried beans generally need a little longer.

STIR-FRIED MANGETOUTS (SNOW PEAS)

Mangetouts are ideal for stir-frying, since they cook very quickly by presenting a large surface area to the heat of the wok. They are tossed in peanut oil flavoured with sliced garlic and finished in a little oyster or soy sauce. Serve them with any Oriental fish or poultry dish and plain boiled rice.

450g/1lb mangetouts, washed
2fl oz/4 tbs peanut oil
4 cloves of garlic, peeled and sliced
8 canned water chestnuts, rinsed and thinly sliced
1fl oz/2 tbs Shaohsing wine or dry sherry
1fl oz/2 tbs oyster or light soy sauce

Trim the ends off the mangetouts. Heat a wok and add the oil. When it starts to smoke, add the garlic and water chestnuts. Stir once and quickly add the mangetouts and stir-fry them for a minute. Add the Shaohsing wine or sherry. Toss for 45 seconds and add the oyster or soy sauce. Stir and serve at once. (Do not exceed the short cooking time or the vegetables will lose their crispness.)

STIR-FRIED BEAN SPROUTS

. . . .

Another versatile and nutritious accompaniment to most Chinese or Thai dishes, bean sprouts are here stir-fried with a little garlic and chilli bean sauce, just one of the many products of the soy bean that are indispensable in Oriental cooking.

1¹/₂fl oz/3 tbs peanut oil
2 cloves of garlic, peeled and sliced
2 spring onions (scallions), washed and sliced
350g/12oz fresh bean sprouts
1 tsp chilli bean sauce
1fl oz/2 tbs water
1 tsp salt

Heat a wok and pour in the oil. When it starts to smoke, add the garlic and white spring onions. Stir. Add the bean sprouts and stir. Add the chilli bean sauce and stir-fry for another minute. Moisten with the water, season and serve.

PINTO BEANS WITH AVOCADO

These speckled beans have acquired their name from the Spanish verb *pintar* (to paint). Serve this salad of beans and avocado as a meal in itself. The various textures are contrastingly soft and crunchy.

350g/12oz dried pinto beans
1 red onion, peeled and thinly sliced
2 cloves of garlic, peeled and finely chopped
2 ripe avocadoes, peeled and cubed
3 fresh green chillies, washed and thinly sliced
1fl oz/2 tbs wine vinegar
110ml/4fl oz/$^1/_2$ cup extra virgin olive oil
generous pinch of dried oregano
$^1/_2$ cup of parsley, washed and chopped
2 carrots, peeled and coarsely grated
1 stick celery, washed and sliced

Soak the pinto beans overnight. Drain and bring them and plenty of water to the boil in a large pot. Simmer, removing the scum, for up to 1½ hours (until soft). Drain and combine in a large bowl with the remaining ingredients, mixing well. Serve when the salad has cooled to room temperature.

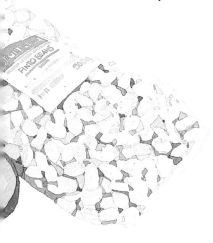

CHICKEN WITH CHICK PEAS

· · · · · · · · · · ·

A substantial and very nourishing stew.

2fl oz/4 tbs olive oil
1 free-range or corn-fed chicken, in serving pieces
1 medium onion, peeled and thinly sliced
1 stick of celery, diced
1 carrot, peeled and diced
175g/6oz mushrooms, thickly sliced
4 cloves of garlic, peeled and chopped
400g/14oz canned plum tomatoes, chopped
225ml/8fl oz/1 cup red wine
2 bay leaves
salt
freshly milled black pepper
450g/1lb can of chick peas
handful of fresh parsley,
washed and chopped

Heat the oil in a heavy, lidded casserole and fry the chicken pieces, turning them until they are evenly golden. Remove and drain them on a paper towel.

Add the onion, celery, and carrot and sauté until they begin to colour. Put in the mushrooms and the garlic, reduce heat, and sauté gently for 3 minutes. Return the chicken pieces to the pan, pour in the chopped tomatoes and the red wine and bring to the boil. Put in the bay leaves, season, reduce the heat, and cover. Simmer gently for 20 minutes.

Meanwhile, rinse and drain the chick peas. Add them to the chicken and simmer uncovered for 5 minutes (boil off excess liquid if necessary). Add the parsley. Simmer for 2 minutes longer and serve.

GRILLED (BROILED) CHICKEN BREASTS WITH SPICY BEANS

· · · · · · · · · · ·

4 chicken breasts
110ml/4fl oz/$^1/_2$ cup fruity olive oil
freshly milled black pepper
juice of 1 lemon
2 cloves of garlic, peeled and crushed
425g/15oz canned borlotti beans
1 small onion, peeled and chopped
1 clove of garlic, peeled and finely chopped
small piece of fresh ginger, peeled and finely chopped
1 tsp sugar
$^1/_2$ dried red chilli, crumbled
2 ripe tomatoes, skinned and diced
3fl oz/6 tbs white wine
salt
freshly milled black pepper
handful of fresh parsley,
washed and chopped

Put the chicken breasts and all but 1fl oz/2 tbs of the olive oil in a bowl and grind black pepper over them. Mix in the lemon juice and add the crushed garlic cloves. Turn to coat and leave for 1 hour.

Rinse the beans well and drain them. Heat the remaining oil in a pan and add the onions. Sauté them for 2 minutes, then add the chopped garlic, ginger, sugar, and chilli. Stir and after another minute add the beans, tomatoes, and wine. Season, reduce the heat and simmer for 15 minutes (cover if the sauce begins to dry out). Add the parsley.

Meanwhile, pre-heat a grill (broiler) or a cast-iron griddle on top of the stove. Take the chicken out of the marinade and grill for 6–8 minutes on each side, or until golden. Serve with the beans and a salad.

RE-FRIED BEANS WITH
TORTILLAS AND SALSA
· · · · · · · · · · ·

Another example of the natural instinct shown by some traditional cuisines, in this case, Mexican for pairing beans with carbohydrate to produce a highly nutritious, protein-rich superfood. Ready-made corn tortillas are available from supermarkets and other food shops. Re-fried beans are widely consumed in Mexico, where beans are an important staple.

800g/1³/₄ lb canned red kidney beans
2fl oz/4 tbs olive oil
1 onion, peeled and chopped
salt
freshly milled black pepper
a few drops of Tabasco sauce (to taste)
450g/1lb canned tomatoes, chopped
2 cloves of garlic, peeled and sliced
1 fresh chilli, sliced
1 tbs red wine vinegar
pinch of thyme and oregano
1fl oz/2 tbs olive oil
salt
freshly milled black pepper
4 tortillas
75g/3oz hard cheese, coarsely grated

Rinse and drain the kidney beans and heat in a small pan with a little fresh water for about 15 minutes. Drain and mash them to a pulp.

Heat the oil in a well-seasoned or non-stick frying pan and put in the onion. Sauté gently for 6–8 minutes, until lightly browned. Add the mashed beans, season with salt, pepper, and Tabasco and fry them, turning them in the pan, until they begin to form a crust.

Meanwhile, make a *salsa* by heating the tomatoes in another pan with the garlic, chilli, red wine vinegar, herbs, oil, and seasoning and cook, for about 15 minutes.

To serve, heat the tortillas in a moderate oven, spoon a generous layer of re-fried beans over each, topped with *salsa* and grated cheese. Serve, accompanied by a rudimentary salad of shredded cos (romaine) lettuce and fresh sliced tomatoes, dressed with extra virgin olive oil and red wine vinegar.

COTECHINO SAUSAGE WITH LENTILS

This very satisfying combination of mild, lightly spiced sausage served with earthy lentils is a speciality of northern Italy, and of Emilia Romagna in particular. Commercial brands of pre-cooked sausage *(cotechino cotto)* can be bought vacuum-packed in good Italian delicatessens. These require only 30 minutes' boiling. Alternatively, prepare commercially made *zampone* (a pig's trotter stuffed with spiced sausage meat) in the same way. Serve the sausage on a serving platter in overlapping slices about 1cm/$\frac{1}{2}$ inch thick, with some mashed potatoes on one side, the lentils on the other. To complete the picture, serve some mustard separately.

225g/8oz green lentils
1 cotechino sausage
2fl oz/4 tbs olive oil
3 cloves of garlic, peeled and chopped
1 medium carrot, peeled and diced
1 stick of celery, washed and diced
2 bay leaves
110ml/4 fl oz/$\frac{1}{2}$ cup water
salt
freshly milled black pepper

Wash the lentils and put them in a pot with enough water to give a 2cm/1 inch covering. Bring to the boil, reduce the heat and simmer them for 15–20 minutes, skimming them from time to time.

Meanwhile, boil the sausage in plenty of water, without removing it from the vacuum pack. (Check the pack instructions: the cooking time should not exceed 35 minutes.)

Heat the oil in another pan and sauté the garlic, carrot, and celery for 5 minutes. Add to the pot with the lentils which should be dry. Add the bay leaves and a little more water, but not enough to cover the lentils, cover and continue to simmer them for 15–20 more minutes. Season well and remove the bay leaves.

With scissors, open the sausage pack and pour off the liquid. Remove the sausage, slice it into 1cm/½ inch sections and serve.

BOSTON BAKED BEANS

· · · · · · · · · · ·

A famous toast proposed by John Collins Bossidy at the Holy Cross Alumni Dinner in 1910 attested:

And this is good old Boston,
The home of the bean and the cod

Boston is another name for haricot (navy) beans.

225g/8oz dried haricot beans
175g/6oz lean bacon, in a piece or cubed
1 whole onion, peeled
1 tbs brown sugar
1 tbs maple syrup
1 tbs mustard
2 cloves
salt
freshly milled black pepper
2 bay leaves
2 tbs tomato paste

Soak the beans overnight in cold water. Drain. Pre-heat an oven to 150°C/300°F/gas mark 2.

Put the beans in a casserole or earthenware pot and add the remaining ingredients, mixing them well. Boil enough water to just cover and pour over the contents. Bake until the beans are really soft (5 or 6 hours), replenishing with more boiling water, if necessary. (Check seasoning before serving.)

OKRA

. . . .

Now relatively easy to buy fresh in markets and supermarkets, okra is a popular pod vegetable in many hot countries and in the southern states of America, where it is known as *gumbo* (both names have obvious African origins). It is especially appreciated in the Middle East and in India, where it is known as *bhindi*. Here are two different ways of cooking okra, the first with Indian spices, the second in a style more typical of the Middle East, where it is usually served warm or at room temperature.

Braised okra

350g/12oz okra, washed and patted dry
1 small onion, peeled and chopped
4 cloves of garlic, peeled and chopped
2 green chillies, washed
$1^{1}/_{2}$ fl oz/3 tbs plus 350ml/12fl oz/$1^{1}/_{2}$ cups water
2 tsp cumin seeds
2 tsp coriander seeds
1 tsp black peppercorns
1 tsp fennel seeds
1 tsp turmeric
$^{1}/_{2}$ tsp cayenne
2fl oz/4 tbs sunflower or corn oil
4 tbs chopped tomatoes
salt

Top and tail the okra. Put the onion, garlic, and green chillies into a food processor with 1 1/2 fl oz/3 tbs of water and process to a paste. Grind the whole dry spices in a coffee grinder or mortar. Mix in the turmeric and cayenne.

Heat the oil in a wide pot or wok and fry the paste until it colours a little, about 2 minutes. Add the okra and turn them around to pick up some of the paste. Add the ground spices and chopped tomatoes and fry for 3–4 more minutes, stirring constantly. Season. Pour in the rest of the water, bring to a simmer, and cook for 25 minutes, or until the okra are tender.

Okra stewed with tomatoes

450g/1lb fresh okra, washed and patted dry
2 fl oz/4 tbs olive oil
4 cloves of garlic, peeled and thinly sliced
1 medium onion, peeled and roughly chopped
400g/14oz canned tomatoes, chopped
2 fl oz/4 tbs water
1 dried red chilli
2 tsp ground coriander seeds
1 tsp sugar
salt
freshly milled black pepper
juice of a lemon

Top and tail the okra.

Heat the oil in a large frying pan and sauté the garlic and onion in it until they begin to colour. Add the okra and sauté for 2–3 more minutes. Add the tomatoes, water, chilli, coriander, and sugar. Stir and bring to the boil. Season, cover and simmer for 20 minutes. Add the lemon juice and simmer for 5 more minutes. Allow to cool before serving.

BABY AUBERGINES (EGGPLANT) IN BLACK BEAN SAUCE

· · · · · · · · · ·

These aromatic baby aubergines can accompany any light stir-fried chicken, beef, or seafood dish as a side vegetable, as long as the other dish does not also include black or another fermented bean paste or sauce. Black beans, which are preserved whole soy beans, are available in Chinese stores, usually in labelled plastic bags but also canned. Very rich in protein, their use is invariably as a seasoning. Substitute 2 large, ordinary aubergines, cut into wedges if the small varieties are unobtainable.

350g/12oz whole baby aubergines, washed and trimmed
50g/2oz fermented black beans, rinsed and drained
1 tsp cayenne
1 tsp peanut oil
1fl oz/2 tbs peanut oil
2 cloves of garlic, peeled and sliced
2 spring onions (scallions), sliced
1 cm/$^{1}/_{2}$ inch piece of fresh ginger, peeled and thinly sliced
1 tsp sugar
$^{1}/_{2}$ tsp salt
225ml/8fl oz/1 cup water
handful of fresh coriander (cilantro), washed and chopped
1 tbs sesame oil

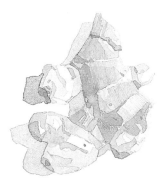

Slice each baby aubergine diagonally, once (leave the
smallest ones whole). Mash the black beans with the
back of a spoon. Mix the cayenne with the black beans
and the teaspoon of oil.

Heat the remaining oil in a wok until smoking, add
the garlic, white spring onion and ginger and stir quickly . Add the aubergine pieces and stir-fry for a minute
before adding the black bean paste. Turn the aubergines around in the paste, then add the sugar and salt
and mix. Continue to cook for another minute. Pour in
the water and simmer on a low heat for 15 minutes. (If
the aubergines dry out, add a little more water.)
Transfer the contents of the wok to a heated serving
dish and sprinkle with the coriander and green spring
onion. Dribble with the sesame oil and serve hot.

FRESH TAGLIATELLE WITH PEAS
· · · · · · · · · · ·

Fresh pasta can be very good if bought from a repu-
table establishment that makes it daily on the
premises. Alternatively it is very easy to make your
own, without a pasta machine.

Tagliatelle

250g/9oz/1 1/2 cups plain (all-purpose) flour
3 eggs
pinch of salt

Put the ingredients into the bowl of a food processor and knead. This can be done very quickly on normal speed: the dough will roll up into a ball. Stop a few seconds after this happens. Let the dough rest for 20 minutes. Flour a large, clean wooden work surface (an old kitchen table is ideal, as long as you don't mind scarring it). Flour the surface of a large rolling pin. Work the dough into a large, very thin sheet. Trim off the ends to form an oblong and gently cut the sheet into long, very narrow strips. Drape these over the back of a chair and let them dry for 20 minutes or so. Boil in salted water for 3 minutes.

Fresh pea sauce

225g/8oz fresh (or frozen) peas (shelled weight)
110ml/4fl oz/$^1/_2$ cup extra virgin olive oil
4 slices of lean bacon, trimmed and diced
small onion, peeled and finely chopped
110g/4oz oyster or shiitake mushrooms, sliced
salt
freshly milled black pepper
110ml/4fl oz/$^1/_2$ cup dry white wine
handful of fresh parsley, washed and chopped
freshly grated parmesan cheese

Shell the peas.

Heat 2fl oz/4 tbs of the oil and fry the bacon until it just starts to brown. Add the onion and soften it. Add the peas and mushrooms and sauté them for 6 minutes. Season, pour in the wine and allow it partly to evaporate, about 3 minutes, then mix in the parsley. Combine well with the pasta and serve with the remaining extra virgin olive oil and parmesan cheese.

PASTA E FAGIOLI
· · · · · · · · · · ·

A famous Tuscan pasta dish for which there are many different recipes. Ideally this should be made with fresh borlotti beans, which may be hard to obtain (their season is late summer) but flageolet beans would also work well. If using fresh beans, simply boil them first in salted water for half an hour. However, to enjoy the dish at any time of the year, it can be made very successfully with canned borlotti or cannellini beans, as suggested here.

2fl oz/4 tbs fruity olive oil
2 slices of lean bacon, trimmed and diced
1 medium onion, peeled and chopped
1 stick of celery, washed and sliced
1 carrot, peeled and diced
2 cloves of garlic, peeled and chopped
425g/15oz can of beans, rinsed and drained
110ml/4fl oz/$^1/_2$ cup dry white wine
pinch of thyme
280g/10oz canned tomatoes, crushed
560ml/1 pint good quality chicken stock (broth)
salt
freshly milled black pepper
75g/3oz small dried pasta shapes (*ditalli, penne, ziti* or
tubetti)
extra virgin olive oil

Heat the oil in a pot and brown the bacon in it. Add
the onions, to soften them, then add the celery and carrots. Continue to sauté the ingredients for 5–6 minutes,
then add the garlic and beans and mix well. Pour in the
wine and let it almost boil away, then add the thyme,
tomatoes, and stock. Season, bring to the boil, and drop
in the pasta. Cook, uncovered for 11 minutes. Remove
from the heat and rest for 5 minutes before serving,
generously anointed with extra virgin olive oil.

LENTIL SOUP

· · · · · · · · · · ·

Lentil soup is one of the more universal of potages. This version is thick and earthy, really filling and nourishing.

2fl oz/4 tbs olive oil
1 medium onion, chopped
3 large carrots, peeled and chopped
2 stalks of celery, washed and chopped
225g/8oz brown lentils, washed and picked over
1600ml/2³/₄ pints of chicken stock (broth)
salt
freshly milled black pepper

Heat the oil in a large, steep-sided pot and fry the onion for 2–3 minutes. Add the carrots and celery and sauté them for 5 minutes. Add the lentils, sauté in the oil for 1 minute more and add the hot stock. Bring to the boil, then partially cover and simmer for 50 minutes or until the lentils are soft. Season to taste and leave the soup to cool, then liquidize in a food processor. Add a little extra stock to thin the soup, if necessary. Reheat without boiling and serve with croûtons. Note: the soup will tend to thicken as time passes. It will keep for a day or two but will need to be further diluted with water or stock and reheated.

SPLIT PEA AND HAM SOUP
· · · · · · · · · · ·

The flavours of dried split peas and ham or bacon combine to produce a marvellous, robust soup. The consistency should be thick and the flavour earthy and intense. There is no need to soak the split peas: just wash and drain them. Green or yellow split peas are equally suitable.

225g/8oz split peas
2 potatoes, peeled and diced
water
salt
2fl oz/4 tbs extra virgin olive oil
75g/3oz lean, thickly cut ham, *or*
lean bacon, trimmed and diced
1 medium onion, finely chopped
1350ml/2½ pints good quality or
home-made chicken stock
(broth)
2 bay leaves
pinch of dried thyme
salt
freshly milled black pepper

Put the peas and potatoes in a pot with salted water to cover them and bring to the boil. Cook, removing the scum, until both have softened (about 20 minutes). Remove and drain them, discarding the cooking liquid.

Heat the olive oil in another pot and brown the ham or bacon, then add the onion. Reduce the heat and soften the onions for about 5 minutes. Add the drained peas and potatoes, the stock, bay leaves and the pinch of thyme. Bring them to the boil, then reduce the heat and simmer, partially covered, for about an hour, stirring occasionally. Season well and simmer for 10–15 minutes longer, stirring often. The peas and potatoes should have melted into the soup, which should be fairly thick. Serve with crusty bread.

FASOULADA

The Greeks have an enduring passion for dried and fresh beans, and this is a typical Greek bean soup.

450g/1lb dried haricot (navy) beans
110ml/4fl oz/$^1/_2$ cup fruity olive oil
2 large onions, peeled and chopped
2 carrots, peeled and diced
2 sticks of celery, diced
4 cloves of garlic, peeled
2 bay leaves
parsley
2 tbs tomato paste
1 tbs white wine vinegar
1350ml/2$^1/_2$ pints of water
salt
freshly milled black pepper

Soak the haricot beans overnight in a large pot of water.

Drain them and bring plenty of water to the boil in the same large pot. Put in the beans and cook them until they are soft, about 1$^1/_2$ hours, then drain.

Heat the olive oil in another large pot and add the chopped onion, carrot, celery, garlic, bay leaves, and parsley. Fry for 2 minutes, then add the beans and stir them in the oil a few times. Add the tomato paste, vinegar, and the water. Season, bring to the boil, cover and simmer for 20 minutes. Check seasoning and serve, adding a few drop of extra virgin olive oil, if you like.

Fasoulia
· · · · · · · · · · ·

I n Greece dried haricot (navy) beans are prepared as soups and in a variety of other ways, including this very popular dish, which is ideal as a light lunch. Serve with bread.

575g/1¼lb dried haricot beans
110ml/4fl oz/½ cup fruity olive oil
1 medium red onion, finely chopped
2 cloves of garlic, peeled and chopped
1 stick of celery, diced
4 slices of bacon or cured ham, diced
1 small dried red chilli pepper, crumbled (optional)
400g/14oz can of plum tomatoes, crushed
splash of water or white wine
salt
freshly milled black pepper
a few leaves of basil

Soak the beans overnight in a large pot of water. Drain, and put them back in the pot with plenty of water. Bring to the boil and simmer them until soft, about 1¼ hours. Drain well.

Heat the oil in a large pan that will accommodate the cooked beans. When it is hot, add the onions, stir for a minute, then add the garlic, celery, and bacon. Sauté for about 3 minutes, then add the chilli (if using), tomatoes, cooked beans and water or white wine. Cover and simmer for 10 minutes. Season well and sprinkle with basil.

RUSTIC BEAN STEW
············

This hearty winter warmer can be served with a crusty bread or polenta. It is easy to make with canned borlotti or cannellini beans.

12g/^{1}/$_2$oz dried porcini mushrooms
2 × 425g/15oz cans beans
2fl oz/4 tbs extra virgin olive oil
2 slices of bacon or cured ham, diced
1 medium onion, peeled and chopped
1 carrot, peeled and chopped
1 stick of celery, washed and sliced
2 cloves of garlic, peeled and chopped
2 bay leaves
400g/14oz canned plum tomatoes, crushed
140ml/5fl oz/^{2}/$_3$ cup dry white wine
salt
freshly milled black pepper
handful of fresh parsley, washed and chopped

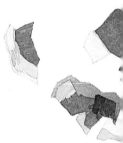

Put the mushrooms in a cup of warm water, to soak for 15 minutes. Rinse and drain the beans.

Heat the oil in a heavy pot with the bacon or ham. Add the onions, carrot, celery and beans. Mix well and fry for 3 or 4 minutes, or until the bacon colours a little. Add the garlic and bay leaves and stir for another minute. Pour in the tomatoes and add the white wine, the mushrooms, and their strained soaking liquid. Season well and mix. Turn heat to low, cover and simmer for 20 minutes, checking that the beans do not become too dry: rectify by adding a little water. Sprinkle with the parsley and serve after the pot has rested for a few minutes.

FUL MEDAMES

The Egyptian national dish that is also enjoyed in many other Middle Eastern countries. A small brown variety of the broad (fava) bean, *ful medames* are usually available dried or in cans. Substitute regular broad beans if the correct variety are unavailable.

500g/18oz dried *ful medames*, or
2 × 425g/15oz cans, rinsed and drained
1 tsp cumin, ground
3 cloves of garlic, peeled and finely chopped
2–3 chopped tomatoes
generous handful of fresh parsley, washed and chopped
110ml/4fl oz/¹/₂ cup extra virgin olive oil
juice of a lemon
salt
freshly milled black pepper
yolks of 2 hard-boiled (hard-cooked) eggs, chopped
1 red onion, peeled and thinly sliced

Soak the dried beans overnight. Drain and bring them to the boil in a large pot of water. Simmer them until soft, about 2 hours, and drain them. (If using pre-cooked, canned beans, rinse well and simmer them in a little water for 10 minutes, then drain.)

Transfer the beans to a serving bowl and combine them with the remaining ingredients and serve warm or cold.

TUSCAN BEANS
· · · · · · · · · · ·

The Tuscans eat prodigious quantities of beans, prepared in a great variety of ways. So dedicated to the
legume are they that their compatriot Italians, most of
whom share a certain fondness for beans and lentils,
refer to them as *mangeafagioli*, or 'bean-eaters'. Here are
two of the many Tuscan ways with beans. In the first
recipe, canned cannellini, red kidney or borlotti beans can
be substituted: omit the soaking, rinse the contents of 2
× 450g/1lb cans well and proceed as if using pre-soaked
and cooked beans. When in season, the second recipe can
be made with fresh borlotti beans, or with the pre-cooked
version available canned.

Fagioli al uccelletto

575g/1¹/₄lb dried haricot (navy) beans
110ml/4fl oz/¹/₂ cup extra virgin olive oil
4–6 fresh sage leaves
1 dried red chilli pepper, crumbled
4 cloves of garlic, peeled and lightly crushed
salt
freshly milled black pepper
4 chopped plum tomatoes, fresh or canned
110ml/4fl oz/¹/₂ cup water

Soak the dried beans overnight and drain them. Put
them and plenty of water in a pot and bring to the boil.
Simmer for 1 hour, or until soft. Drain them well.

Heat half of the oil in a large pan or casserole and
simmer the sage, chilli and the garlic cloves until they
are lightly coloured. Add the beans, stir them well to
coat, season, and add the tomatoes and water. Cover
and simmer for 25 minutes. Drizzle with the remaining oil and serve.

Bean and vegetable Soup

The ingredients listed below are a suggestion only: other seasonal vegetables can be substituted, with equal success.

450g/1lb mixed leaf vegetables
(swiss chard, cabbage, spinach)
450g/1lb fresh borlotti beans, shelled *or*
225g/8oz canned
225g/8oz broccoli or cauliflower florets
1 large carrot, finely diced
1 stick of celery, sliced
1 medium onion, peeled and chopped
2 cloves of garlic, peeled and chopped
2–3 courgettes (zucchini), diced
1 potato, peeled and diced
salt
freshly milled black pepper
1350ml/2½ pints water
4 slices of stale, hard bread

Shred the leaf vegetables. Combine with the remaining ingredients except the bread and canned beans in a large pot with the water. (If using canned beans, rinse, drain, and add them 15 minutes before the end of the cooking time.)

Bring the pot to a simmer, cover, and cook the soup for 2 hours. Check the seasoning. Allow to cool a little and serve, pouring the thick liquid into four bowls into which you have placed the stale bread. If you like, dribble a little extra virgin olive oil into the soup. It is even better re-heated.

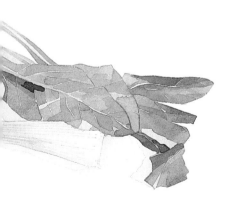

RISI E BISI
· · · · · · · · · · ·

This famous Venetian dish combining fresh peas and rice is exceptionally nutritious and rich in protein. In this case a little butter is essential, but the quantity is not great. Such is the simplicity of *risi e bisi* (neither a soup nor a risotto but a combination of the two) that only the best ingredients – small, tender, fresh peas, Italian arborio rice, real parmesan cheese, and good quality stock (broth) – will produce the desired results.

900g/2lb peas in their shells
50g/2oz unsalted butter
1 fl oz/2 tbs sunflower oil
1 medium onion, chopped
1120ml/2¼ pints home-made chicken stock
225g/8oz/1 cup arborio rice
½ cup of fresh parsley, washed and chopped
salt
freshly milled black pepper
110g/4oz piece of parmesan, grated

Shell the peas.

Heat half the butter and the oil in a large, heavy pan. Soften the onion and before it browns (about 3 minutes) add the stock, rice, and parsley; season, and boil over a medium heat for 30 minutes. After 15 minutes, add the peas and cover, to prevent the stock from boiling away. Stir occasionally. Mix in the remaining butter and parmesan and serve.

STOCK (BROTH)

Because some of the recipes in this book call for home-made stock, here are two simple recipes, one for chicken, the other for vegetable stock.

1 uncooked, skinned chicken carcass
2 large onions, peeled and quartered
2 large carrots, peeled and roughly chopped
1 large stick of celery, roughly chopped
bunch of fresh parsley (stalks and leaves)
12 black peppercorns
2 bay leaves
salt
2 litres/3^1/$_2$ pints water

Put all the ingredients into a very large pot and bring to a boil. Cover, reduce the heat, and simmer, skimming off the scum from time to time. After 2 hours, the stock will be ready. Allow it to cool, remove any surplus fat and refrigerate or pour into freezer bags and store in the freezer until required. To thaw, pour boiling water over the frozen stock and carefully peel away the bag. Put the block of frozen stock into a pot, cover, and simmer until completely melted.

To make vegetable stock combine in a large pot 2fl oz/4 tbs of olive oil, 2 peeled onions, 2–3 leeks, 3 carrots, 5–6 celery stalks, a parsnip, 2 tomatoes, some parsley stalks with their leaves, 1 tbs tomato paste, salt, freshly milled black pepper, and 2 litres/3^1/$_2$ pints of water. Bring to the boil, stir well, cover, reduce the heat and simmer for 1^1/$_2$ hours. Re-season. Store as above.